Selected Churches of Dublin

Joe Curtis

First Edition, 2012

Distributed by: www.amazon.com

© Copyright. Joe Curtis. 2012.

Front Cover: East window of Christ Church, Bray

Introduction

Various books deal with the Catholic churches in Dublin, and the two Protestant cathedrals, but information is scarce about the Protestant churches, comprising Anglican, Presbyterian, Methodist and Evangelical. The Quaker, Brethren, and Orthodox churches, all branches of Christianity, are also neglected, and likewise other minority religions, such as Islam and Judaism. Very often, these churches and places of worship are only open for about one hour a week, and therefore the general public and visitors never get the chance to look inside. This book is not about religion, nor architecture, but simply provides a snapshot of the inside of the churches, together with some basic background information.

Unless otherwise stated, all of the churches listed here are Anglican, another name for Church of Ireland. Some members call themselves "reformed Catholics", since their ancestors were all Catholics, and protested at abuses in the Catholic Church, prompting the Reformation in the early part of the 16th century, and a new status as Protestants ("Protestors"). Unfortunately, most of the Protestants in Ireland were also "settlers", that is, ordinary English people who were encouraged to emigrate from England to Ireland, and become tenants on the large landed estates which had been confiscated from the native Irish after various wars. So the Protestant religion, while being very progressive and worthy in its own right, was seen by the Irish as a British way of gaining control over the country. Nevertheless, all Protestants are Christians, sharing the same core values as Catholics. Contrary to popular belief, Protestants in Ireland nowadays come from all social backgrounds, including a sizable working class.

There are some Anglican churches in Dublin known as "High Church", meaning that their Sunday Services are very similar to that in the old Catholic churches, especially before Vatican II.

Many Irish people have never been inside a Protestant church, partly because the Catholic hierarchy forbade its flock from having anything to do with that religion. Therefore, native visitors will tend to compare the inside with their own Catholic church, and will notice the absence of confessional boxes, statues, and "Stations of the Cross". However, very prominent in most Protestant churches are memorials to deceased parishioners, usually local landlords and benefactors, some in fact in the form of busts or even statues. Also in evidence will be World War 1 and 2 memorials, listing deceased Protestant parishioners (never their Catholic comrades), although some people think that such items would be better in cemeteries.

Quite a few of the churches included here started as smaller simple buildings, but the congregations over the many generations spent a lot of time fundraising for numerous extensions and alterations, so that the original building is sometimes completely changed.

The reference to "chapel of ease" should not be confused with the term "chapel". Prior to Catholic Emancipation in 1829, the state sponsored religion in Ireland was the Church of Ireland, also called Anglicans. Their places of worship were called churches, and hence were usually located in a street named Church Street, especially in the towns and villages around Ireland. The Catholics worshipped in chapels, often located in Chapel Street. Prior to Dis-Establishment in 1869, the Anglican Church was also the forerunner of local Government, and appointed the local Constable.

Many of the churches featured are faced with granite, a symbol of strength and longevity. A substantial number are built of squared limestone, although the older ones are sometimes of rough local limestone, known as black calp limestone, either bare or with smooth rendering (plaster). Very few churches are built of brick. Frequently, another stone, such as sandstone or limestone, is introduced to elevations in the form of "dressings", around windows, at quoins (corners), or as tracery in big windows. Roofs are usually covered with natural slates. Many of the churches would feel quite small inside if they had flat plastered ceilings, but

4

instead, the roof structure is used as a feature, to give added height internally. Frequently, the roof structure consists of different variations of the "arch brace", so that the higher regions of the church are free of all timberwork. However, there are quite a few more complicated roof trusses, such as "scissor trusses", "king post trusses". "queen post trusses", and occasionally a "hammer beam truss", some carved, and all nicely stained and varnished.

Most of the churches have a few lovely stained glass windows, works of art in their own right, some imported from Germany, France and England, although a high percentage are by Irish artists, especially from the famous studio called "An Tur Gloinne" (The Tower of Glass), and also a few by Harry Clarke or his father's studio, Joshua Clarke & Sons. An Tur Gloinne was founded at 24 Upper Pembroke Street, in 1903, by Sarah Purser and Edward Martyn, and most of the artists had trained in the Metropolitan School of Art at the rear of the National Library (later called the National College of Art and Design), including Catherine O'Brien, Michael Healy, Alfred Ernest Child, Wilhelmina Geddes, Evie Hone, and Ethel Rhind. Windows are often lancet type, in the Gothic style.

Generally speaking, churches are oriented on an east-west axis, with the altar at the east end, facing Jerusalem in Palestine/Israel.

Around the year 1054, the Christian religion split in two, the West being governed by Popes in Rome, and the East governed by a Patriarch in Constantinople (now called Istanbul) - the latter came to be known as the Orthodox Church, and these days, comprises Russian Orthodox, Greek Orthodox, etc.

In Dublin on a Sunday morning, when you hear a church bell, it is usually from a Catholic or an Orthodox church, and the pealing of a collection of bells is usually from the Protestant cathedrals.

Abbey Street Lr - Dublin Central Mission

Built in 1820, but the Methodists remodelled/rebuilt this church in 1901. The galleries to the sides and rear were enclosed in the 1930's. Could be mistaken for a shop or offices.

Abbey Street Lr - Scots Church

"Scots" immediatly tells you that Scottish Presbyterians built this church, in 1869. The adjoining hall was added in 1886.

The organ usually takes centre-stage in Presbyterian churches.

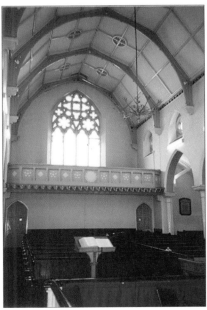

Adelaide Road - Presbyterian

This Presbyterian church dates from 1841, although was rebuilt in 2002, retaining only the facade, and the 1896 organ. Singing, led by the precentor, is a big part of the Presbyterian religion. This building is an excellent example of how churches should be converted to multi-function. In the lower ground floor is a church hall for informal gatherings, a childcare facility, and kitchen. On the ground floor is a multi-purpose foyer, and the Donore Room – the church proper, with accommodation for 200 people. There is a mezzanine space above the church. The first floor is for community use – interview rooms, computer skills, showers, etc. The top floor is laid out as four apartments, for use by staff and the congregation. "Dolebusters" have operated from the building since the 1980's offering adult education and training.

Adelaide Road - St Finnians

When it opened in 1863, it was known as the Catholic Apostolic Church.

The Church of Ireland bought the church in 1933, and in recent years it came into the hands of the Lutheran Church, catering for German residents. Some will recall that Martin Luther in Germany objected to abuses in the Catholic Church, and so started the Reformation to reform the church.

Note the "scissor roof trusses", coupled with a type of "arch brace".

Arbour Hill - Church of the Annunciation

The Greek Orthodox church acquired this neat red-bricked building in 1994. The building was an infant school, built in 1890.

Balbriggan - St George

The church was built in Church Street, in 1816, but following a very serious fire in 1835, was restored, and the transepts added, in addition to a spire. Brown sandstone battlements were added to the tower at the same time. The gallery was added in 1862.

The interior is very spacious, although could be regarded as bleak for a small country town congregation. Memorials of local landlord and patron, Hamilton. One stained glass window by Catherine O'Brien in south transept in the 1950's, and two others by Mayer of Munich.

Note the roof trusses, a variation on the "king post" design, which is almost identical to the roof at Ballybrack, near Killiney.

Ballybrack - St Matthias

This granite church, on Church Road, near Killiney, was built in 1835, on land donated by Sir Compton Domville, to a design by Darley. Transepts added in 1870's, and designed by Welland & Gillespie.

There are many stained glass windows by Mayer of Munich., and one, "St Brigid", by Catherine O'Brien. Interesting "king post" trusses support the roof.

Blackrock - All Saints

This charming and very beautiful church, on Carysfort Avenue, was consecrated in 1870, immediatly after the Anglican churches were Dis-Established by law. Before this, the entire population, including Catholics and Dissenters (Presbyterian, Methodist, etc) paid for the upkeep of the Anglican churches, by way of "tithes", but thereafter, the Anglicans had to be self-sufficient. The architect was John McCurdy, and the church was built by Beckett for £3,044. Granite is the main building material, with some sandstone dressings.

The church has many stained glass windows, including such artists as Wilhelmina Geddes of An Tur Gloinne, Earley & Co of Camden Street, Heaton Butler & Bayne of London, and James Powell & Son of London.

In the baptistry, the St Columba panel, painted by Brigid Ganly in 1936, is very attractive, and the faces are those of real parishioners.

Blackrock - St Andrews

This Presbyterian church on Mount Merrion Avenue, which opened in 1899, was designed by Murray and Forrester of London, in an octagonal shape, faced with granite, with Portland stone dressings. The organ now faces the altar, having been moved in 1949 from its original position on the altar.   The Scots philanthropist, Andrew Carnegie, part funded the purchase of the huge organ in 1912.

Blackrock - Methodist

This neat granite building in Newtown Avenue dates from 1861, and was designed with the church on the first floor, and a girls Intermediate (Secondary) school on the ground floor, doubling up as a Sunday School for religious lessons. The small congregation moved to Dun Laoire in 1998, and the building became known as "Urban Junction", a Christian endeavour to reach out to young people, partly through a disco known as "Bounce". Around 2003, the focus shifted to include adults, and various community activities, include keep-fit classes, crèche, etc. A semi-religious service is held on Sunday evenings for young people, called "Ignite", including music - possibly a pun on the former Fire Station alongside!

Blessington - St Marys

Built by Archbishop Boyle in 1683, although the north and south transepts date from 1856 and 1889 respectively.

The six bells were cast in 1682, and are still rung by "change ringers". One bell is also used by the 1698 clock, reputed to be the oldest working clock in Ireland.

There are original boxed pews on the rear gallery.

There are main "arch brace" roof trusses, interspersed with "scissor" type, all unfortunately painted white.

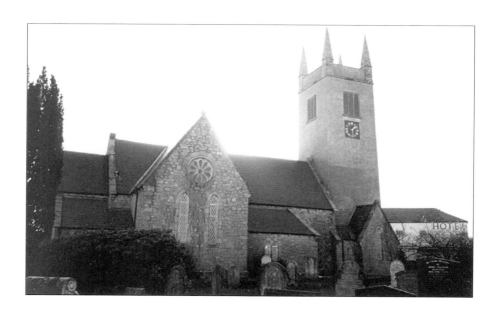

Booterstown - St Philip & St James

This church, on Cross Avenue, was consecrated in 1824, and built on a site provided by the Earl of Pembroke. James Digges La Touche provided the funding for the building work. In 1868 the south transept and chancel were added, while the north transept dates from 1876.

The vaulted ceilings make a pleasant change from the open roofwork of many other churches. There are numerous stained glass windows by Heiton Butler & Bayne of London.

Booterstown

South Hill Evangelical Church has its roots in the Plymouth Brethren, which started in England in the 1820's. This homely building dates from 1953, when the congregation moved from 22 Sydney Avenue in Blackrock, to the top of Booterstown Avenue. Baptism by immersion is reserved for teenagers/adults.

Bray - Christ Church

Consecrated in 1863, and designed by the London architects, Carpenter and Slater. The 175 foot high tower and spire was completed in 1870, and eight Taylor bells were installed about ten years later, ranging in weight from 7 cwt to 1½ ton. There is a lot of English stained glass, including The Last Supper and Ascension in the east window, although the window in the vestry, by Mayer of Munich, is probably the most attractive.

The church, situated on Church Road, looks more like a cathedral, possibly reflecting the involvement of local landlord, the Earl of Meath. Granite is the main external material, although sandstone is used for the aisle pillars inside.

Bray - St Andrews

This cosy Presbyterian church on the corner of Quinsboro Road dates from 1859, but the transepts date from the 1890's. Reputed to have been designed by William Barre. There are some nice stained glass windows, many from Belfast, including a very attractive one in the south transept (curtained-off vestry). The west window has as its centrepiece, the "Burning Bush" from the Old Testament – there is a similar motif in the mosaic floor tiles of the porch. The Star of David or Double Triangle is incorporated in the east window, behind the organ, representing the "Trinity".

Bray - St Andrews

This small Methodist church on the corner of Florence Road was built in 1859, and unusually, shares the same name and date as the nearby Presbyterian church. The exterior comprises granite, with sandstone dressings. There is no stained glass in the narrow lancet windows.

Note the "arch brace" roof trusses, supported on wide corbels. Above the brace arch is a small "king post" truss.

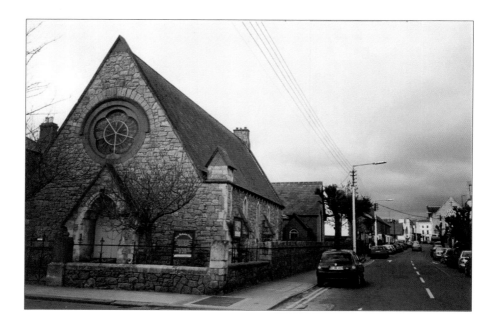

Bray - St Brigids

On the N11 at Kilbride, opposite the turn off for Enniskerry. Dates from 1857, and was designed by William Barre.

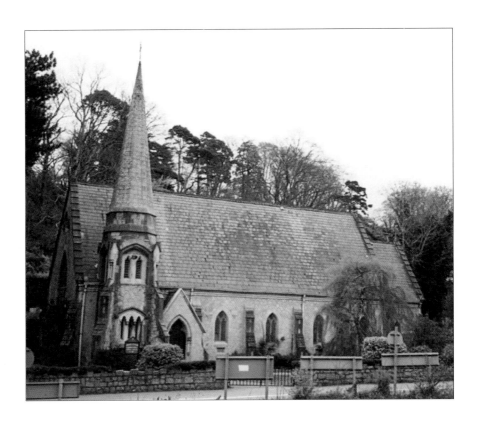

Bray - former St Pauls

Standing on high ground above the River Dargle, opposite the Royal Starlight Hotel, stands the oldest building in Bray, dating from 1609, although partially rebuilt and altered a few times during the 19th century, and again at the beginning of the 20th century (except the crenellated tower, which is substantially original). An old graveyard surrounds the church – an interesting headstone is the one for the Cripples Home in Bray. Most of the exterior is rendered, with granite dressings, although the east traceried window is sandstone. Internally, the "hammer beam" roof trusses are very interesting, including the carved angels on the ends of the beams themselves. Sandstone columns separate the nave from the transepts.

The building was originally the parish church for Bray, until Christ Church was built at the south end of the town. The church was de-consecrated in 1977, and was used for many years by the world-renowned church organ-maker, Kenneth Jones and Associates (who now trade as Kenneth Jones Pipe Organs in nearby Kilcoole). After much voluntary hard work, in 2010 the building was re-opened by the Mountain View Community Church, and called "The Well", a non-denominational Christian church.

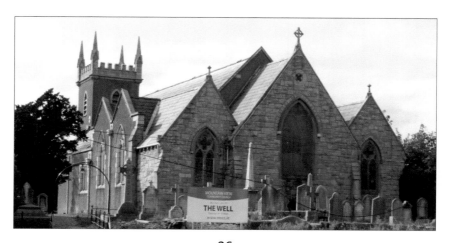

Castleknock - St Brigids

The church, on the Main Street, dates from 1810, built on the site of an early 17th century church, but with 13th century roots. The spire was added in 1864, but had to be removed after being hit by lightning in 1957. The two side aisles and tower do not appear to be original. The exterior is in rubble limestone, with granite dressings.

There are two bells: one cast in 1855, and the other installed in the same year, although was cast in 1747 for St Werburghs near Dublin Castle. There is a 1928 three-light Harry Clarke window on the south side.

The parish includes Aras an Uachtarain in the adjoining Phoenix Park, so a seat is reserved for the President, whether Catholic or Protestant.

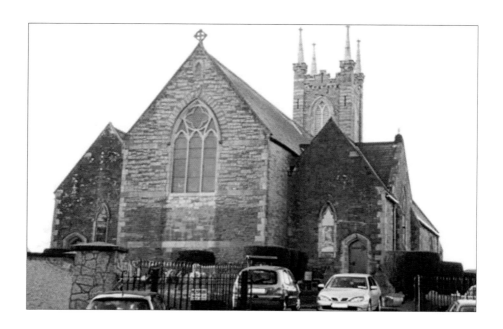

Cathal Brugha Street - St Thomas

Not often do you find brick churches in Dublin, but here is one such, built only in 1931, and designed by Frederick Hicks.

The three stained glass windows in the apse are by Catherine O'Brien.

This church is now shared with the Indian Orthodox congregation, known as the Malankara Prayer Fellowship. The Anglicans have their service first, and then a red curtain is drawn across the apse to convert the altar area into a sacred space.

Chapelizod - St Lawrences

Chapelizod is a very old and interesting village. The church dates from 1832, although the tower is 14th century. The church was remodelled in 1859.

Church Street - St Michans

Possibly the oldest church in Dublin, dating from 1095, although rebuilt/remodelled in 1686, and restored in 1828. The tower is 14th century.

The organ gallery, and the wood carving on the front depicting seventeen musical instruments, dates from 1724. There is a 1909 Catherine O'Brien stained glass window (very early).

The crypt is a famous tourist attraction, because of the preserved "mummies", some with leathery skin affixed.

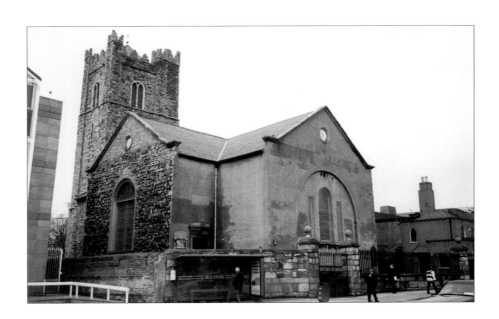

45

Celbridge - Christ Church

Built in 1813 just inside the gate of the Castletown Estate, and rebuilt in 1884, to a design by Thomas Drew. Comprises a nave, chancel, north aisle, and organ chamber. The walls are of limestone, with red sandstone dressings. There is no spire on the tower, which houses two rope-operated bells, still used every Sunday. The organ was previously in a local big house. There are a number of English stained glass windows, and four lancets on the south side of the sanctuary attributed to Watson of Youghal, Co Cork. The carved Last Supper in the white marble reredos is noteworthy. Note also the "hammer beam" roof trusses.

Churchtown - Quakers

Members of the Religious Society of Friends are commonly known as "Quakers", and they practice a simplified form of Christianity, with no priests or rulers. Weekly gatherings are generally for contemplation, or maybe some discussion about the Bible.

This Meeting House, set well back from the Lower Churchtown Road, was purpose-built in 1861, and consists of two front rooms, and a small rear hall.

Clondalkin - St John

Clondalkin is a very old and historic district, as evidenced by the nearby Round Tower. The church was built in 1789, and restored in 1834. Note the "arch brace" roof trusses.

Clonsilla - St MARYS

Built in 1845, and tower added in 1850. Lovely bright Evie Hone window, and others by Joshua Clarke & Sons, and A. E. Child. Note the beautiful ornate roof trusses, of "king post" design., and the "boxed" pews.

Clonskeagh - Mosque

The Islamic Cultural Centre of Ireland was built in 1996 on a four acre site, to a design by Michael Collins Associates, and funded by the deputy ruler of Dubai, Sheikh Hamdan Al Maktoum. It is situated on Roebuck Road, near Bird Avenue.

The focal point is the arched niche, called the mihrab, beside which is the minbar or pulpit, from which the Friday sermon is preached. Their positioning enables worshipers to face east towards Mecca in Saudi Arabia.

There are no seats, and the women pray from the gallery. Shoes are removed by all when entering for prayer. Worshipers must wash beforehand.

54

Clontarf - St John the Baptist

Seafield Road in Dollymount is home to this 1866 church, which replaced a nearby 17th century church. The chancel was added in 1899.

The site was given by John Edward Venables Vernon, who lived in Clontarf Castle, and who was one of the first trustees. The Ecclesiastical Commissioners gave £4,000 of the £6,000 needed to build the church.

The 1866 east window, depicting the twelve apostles, is by O'Connor of London (obviously Irish).

Clyde Road - St Bartholomews

This granite landmark, with sandstone dressings, on a site donated by the Earl of Pembroke, opened in 1867, and was designed by Thomas Henry Wyatt. In 1881 the tower was added, including eight Taylor bells, a four-faced Gillett and Bland clock, and a carillon – the Westminister quarter chime clock brings a sense of peace to Ballsbridge. The service here is regarded as "High church", with a strong emphasis on music and choirs.

The building comprises a nave, transepts, and a long chancel, with the choir and organ in the outer part, and altar in the apse. The nave has "arch brace" roof trusses, all nicely carved and decorated, while there is a flat panelled ceiling over the choir. Murals and mosaic tiles adorn the chancel. Every window has stained glass, including some by Michael O'Connor and Catherine O'Brien.

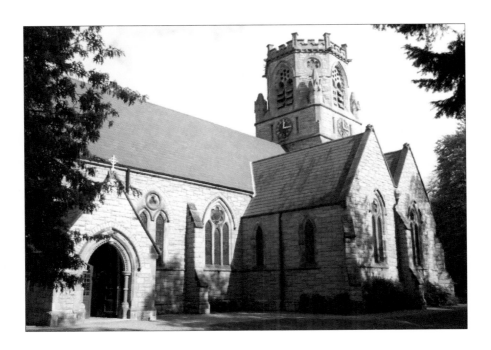

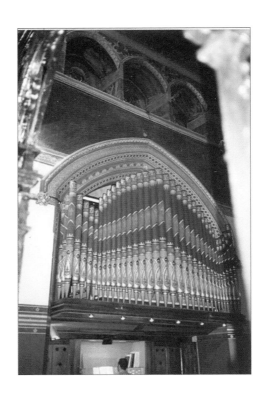

Coolock - St John the Evangelist

Situated on Tonlegee Road, this church dates from 1760, and the tower added about 30 years later, all built on the site of the ruined St Brendans. The transepts and apse date from 1818.

Cornmarket - St Audoen

The side aisle dates from end of 12th century, although restored in 1848, and is still in use. The 17th century tower has six bells, three cast in 1423 (Ireland's oldest), and are still rung by "change ringers".

Crinken - St James

This graceful granite built Trustee church dates from 1840, with the addition of the east chancel in 1882. Before this, Mr Robert McGhee was preaching from small houses in Bray, and was a spiritual adviser to Lord Powerscourt in Enniskerry. With financial backing from two rich ladies, Mrs Magan and Mrs Clarke, a new church was built in Crinken, Shanganagh, near Bray. Mr McGhee by now had been ordained in the Anglican church, but he opted to start his career in Harolds Cross in their new church, which opened in 1838. The large east window has coloured glass, while the nave windows have mostly English stained glass.

Crumlin - St Marys

Probably the last Anglican church to be built in Dublin, dating from 1942, and designed by McDonnell & Dixon. The original 1817 church is abandoned nearby. Both situated at junction of St Mary's and St Agnes Roads.

Dalkey - St Patricks

Overlooking Bullock Harbour, on Harbour Road, this granite church was completed in 1843, to a design by Jacob Owen, and initially called Dalkey Episcopal Chapel of Ease (in Monkstown parish). The quarry site was donated by the Ballast Board. The chancel, with Star of David traceried window, was extended in 1879, to a design by Edward Carson. The church gave up its Trustee status in 1909, and is now under the Representative Church Body. In the mid 1950's, the galleries in the transepts were removed entirely, and the west gallery rebuilt.

The "queen post" roof trusses are highlighted, by plastering the rest of the roof structure.

There are no stained glass windows, except a small panel in the large east window, by Mayer of Munich, entitled "Jesus Blessing the Children".

Dawson Street - St Anns

The 1868 facade (by Sir Thomas Deane) belies an older structure behind, built in the early 1720's. All windows are fitted with stained glass, including some glass by Wilhelmina Geddes and Ethel Rhind. There is a memorial to Sir Hugh Lane, the art collector, who perished in the sinking of the Lusitania in 1915. Behind the altar, the entire reredos comprises a memorial to the War dead, which may not be the most appropriate place.

The "Bread Shelf" is still in use since 1723, where anyone can take a loaf of bread for free – it is on the north side of the chancel/apse.

Deansgrange - Kill O' The Grange

This charming building was a chapel-of-ease for Monkstown parish, and was built in 1864, to a design by Welland & Gillespie. There is one Catherine O'Brien and one McGoldrick stained glass window, in the north wall and apse respectively – the former is signed, and features the logo of An Tur Gloinne above "K.O'B". Note the "wagon" style roof inside.

Delgany - Christ Church

Built in 1789 by Peter La Touche, a French Protestant (Huguenot) who emigrated to Dublin, and achieved fame. David LaTouche, the grandfather of Peter, is commemorated by a giant white marble monument in the church, executed by the renowned John Hickey in 1789. Following a major fire, the church was rebuilt in 1871, and the chancel and vestry added. The chancel is now the organ loft.

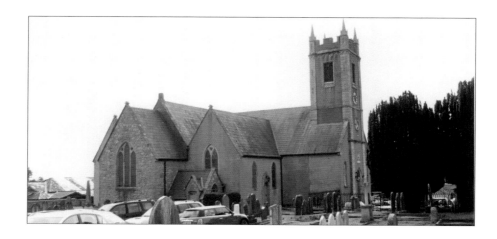

Donabate - St Patricks

Although the church was rebuilt in 1704, (and extended in 1874), the ruined tower beside the north-east corner points to a much older development. A really quaint and interesting church.

The rear gallery has a lovely stucco ceiling, and own fireplace – for the Cobbe family from nearby Newbridge House.

Donnybrook - St Marys

Built of squared black calp limestone in 1827 to a familiar John Semple design. Transepts, chancel and vestry added by Joseph Welland in 1860, using a better limestone. Every second roof truss is an arch brace supporting a scissor truss, while the other trusses are arch brace, all springing off low level granite corbels. In recent decades, two thirds of the nave has been sectioned off by a brick wall to provide a hall, the rear gallery removed, and all walls stripped back to bare rubble calp limestone. On Anglesea Road.

Hall

Donore Avenue - St Catherine & St James

This red brick building is comparatively modern, dating from 1897, but the transepts, chancel, and bell tower were added in 1914, bringing the capacity to 470.

Originally it was called St Catherines Chapel of Ease, being part of St Catherine's parish in Thomas Street. It was renamed St Victor's in 1914. Following the closure in the 1960's of St Catherine's church in Thomas Street, and St James's in James Street, the church in Donore Ave was renamed St Catherines & St James in 1968.

There are three stained glass windows by Michael Healy, and one by Catherine O'Brien, the latter dedicated to St Columba.

Drumcondra - St John the Baptist

Built in 1743 in Church Avenue, and paid for by Miss Coghill, in memory of her brother, Marmaduke Coghill, M.P. The church was located on their estate, Drumcondra House, which was to become All Hallows College a hundred years later.

The cemetery contains the grave of famous architect, James Gandon, and also Francis Grose.

The east window depicts the Ascension in vivid colours, by Earley & Co, of Camden Street, Dublin, in 1901.

Coghill Monument on left.

Dundrum - St Nahi's

Now under the Dargan Luas Bridge, this very small homely church, built of rubble granite, was consecrated in 1760, but was built on the site of an earlier church, dating back to the year 800. Restoration was carried out in 1910/14.

For such a small building, there is a lot of stained glass, mostly from the studios of "An Tur Gloinne" – "The Tower of Glass" – including works by Alfred Ernest Child, Evie Hone, Catherine O'Brien, and Ethel Rhind.

There are four framed panels of embroidery behind the altar, beneath the east window, by Lily and Lolly Yeats, sisters of W.B Yeats and J.B. Yeats.

85

Dun Laoghaire - Christ Church

Built in 1836 as The Bethel Episcopal Free Chapel, a trustee church, dependent on pew rents. After the transepts and chancel were added in 1870, it changed its name to Christ Church. The nave was extended to the rear in 1887, and two years later the church came under the control of the Representative Church Body (RCB). Situated in Park Road, overlooking the Peoples Park.

There are stained glass windows by A.E. Child, and Joshua Clarke of North Frederick Street, the father of the renowned Harry Clarke.

The roof is supported on "scissor" type trusses.

87

Dun Laoghaire - York Road

This Presbyterian church was rebuilt in 1863, replacing the 1828 "Scots Church". The exterior is in granite, with Portland stone dressings. A hall is provided under the church. "Braced arch" and "scissor" trusses support the roof.

Enniskerry - St Patricks

Opened in 1860, but not consecrated until three years later. Lord Powerscourt had his own private chapel inside the nearby demesne.

Stained glass windows by O'Connor, London, from around the time of construction.

Fairview - Presbyterian

Situated at the junction of Clontarf and Howth Roads, this Presbyterian church dates from 1890, being faced with granite, and having red sandstone dressings, giving it a sharp appearance. The tower was added later.

As with many Presbyterian churches, the organ is the focal point in the sanctuary. There is a notable 1919 Harry Clarke window in the west wall, to commemorate parishioners who died in the First World War. Note the "hammer beam" roof trusses.

93

Finglas - St Canices

This church, on Church Street, dates from 1843, replacing a nearby 17th century church, and was designed to hold 220 people. Some memorials from the old church can be seen in the new building. In 1902 a chancel was built, incorporating a stained glass window by Earley & Powell.

Glasnevin - St Mobhi's

The church, on Church Avenue, off Ballymun Road, dates from 1707. However, the tower dates back to the 14th century, and was restored in the 17th century. The vestry was built in 1815, the chancel and organ chamber in 1896, and the south transept in 1908.

The pulpit and organ screen were carved in 1909 by the pupils and staff of Claremont Institute for Deaf and Dumb.

Sir John Rogerson (of Liffey quay fame), a businessman and Lord Mayor, was one of the first wardens.

The big landlord around here was the Lindsay family, and their grave adjoins the church.

The "king post" roof trusses are specially highlighted.

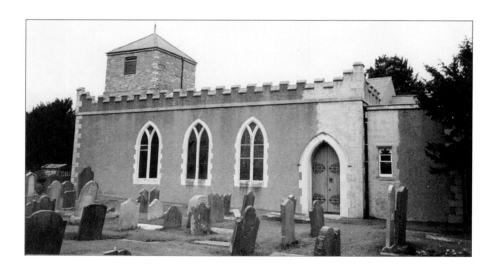

Glenageary - St Pauls

Dating from 1868, St Pauls, on Silchester Road, is built of polygonal granite, with limestone quoins and sandstone window surrounds. The double transept, on the south side, was built in 1898, partly as an organ chamber, when the organ was moved from the chancel. The apse was added to the chancel in 1913. The Trustee church was vested in the RCB in 1918, and pew rents abolished in 1957.

The tower has a peal of nine bells, five cast in 1872, and four in 1877, all by Taylor of Loughborough, from 2½ to 15 cwt, with internal clappers, operated by a chiming frame on the floor below, so that tunes can be played on eight of them, and the large fixed tenor used to call worshipers to service on Sundays.

Note the "jointed cruck" roof trusses, springing from low corbels.

Grangegorman - All Saints

This church is located on Constitution Hill, near Phibsborough, and dates from 1828, to a design by John Semple, with the addition of the chancel in 1856, and the north aisle in 1865.

The 1920 War Memorial tri-panel inside is by Percy Reeves. In 1921 Ethel Rhind from "An Tur Gloinne" studio, made the War Memorial on the outside south elevation.

The grey limestone exterior belies the warm brick interior finish, with contrasting blue band courses. The corbels on the walls point to a previous "arch brace" type roof structure, which was replaced by a simpler collar roof, after a big fire in 1966.

Services are considered "High Church".

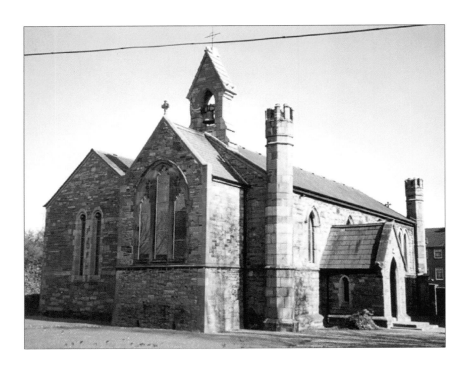

Greystones - St Patrick

Built in 1857 to a design by Welland and Gillespie, on land donated by the La Touche family, and substantially paid for by them. North transept added in 1875, south transept in 1888. The nave was extended, and a gallery installed, in 1898. In 2005, the pews were removed, and replaced by cushioned seats, and carpeting provided throughout. Situated on Church Road.

"Braced arch" trusses support the nave roof, while "hammer beam" trusses are used over the chancel, and "scissor" trusses over the transepts . The exterior consists of greenish rubble stonework, with granite dressings around windows, thereby making it one of the few buildings in Greystones which are unplastered.

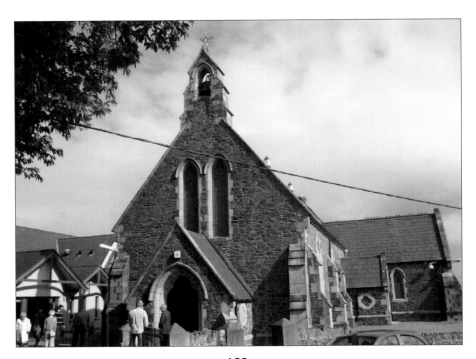

Hardwicke Place - St George

This famous and majestic church was designed by the renowned architect, Francis Johnston, and completed in 1814. The chancel dates from 1880. The proportions are unusual: 84 feet wide by 60 feet deep. The church closed in 1990, and was recently converted into offices. The original bells, presented by the architect as a gift in 1828, were re-hung in 2000 in Taney Church, Dundrum.

Harold's Cross - St Peter & St Paul

The Harolds Cross Episcopal Church was built in 1838 as a Trustee Chapel, with private donations, and specialised in preaching. In 1903 the church was accepted into the Anglican parish system, and amalgamated with Rathmines parish in 1977. The church closed in 2001, because of a dwindling congregation.

The Russian Orthodox community acquired the church in 2002, in time for their Easter ceremonies, although the official consecration did not take place until February 2003. All the pews have been removed to storage, and a beautiful screen (iconostasis – timber covered with paintings of saints, called icons), erected across the sanctuary, to conceal the sacred altar behind. The organ on the rear gallery is not used, because Gregorian plain chant is a special feature of services. The congregation stands for the service, which can last up to two hours.

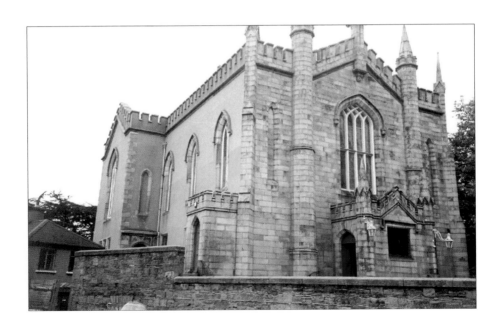

When used by the Church of Ireland

108

Construction of the Orthodox altar behind the screen, containing sacred relics.

Howth - St Marys

Dating from 1866, the building is tucked away inside the entrance to Deerpark. This lovely church hosts a feast of stained glass windows, by such artists as Sarah Purser, Evie Hone, Ethel Rhind, and Catherine O'Brien (who usually signed herself as K.O.B.), all from "An Tur Gloinne" studios. The east window of 1910 is by James Powell & Sons of London.

Howth - Presbyterian

Opposite Claremont Road, this unusual and attractive church dates from 1900, designed by the English architect, Arthur Young, and built by Joseph Small, on Lord Howth's former Deerpark. Before that, the Scots fishermen used the Mariners Hall on the West Pier (which is still standing). The church is built of limestone, with sandstone tracery and window dressings. The plain red tiled roof is uncommon. Clasping buttresses prop up the corners. Orientation is north-south, and over the decades the altar was changed from one end to the other, but in recent years the bench seats have been removed, and the simple altar is now in the centre west. The chancel and organ are incorporated into the three storey tower. The roof inside is a "wagon" type. Originally, there was a gallery in the two low transepts, and also in the north tower area, but these are now gone. There was also a timber spire on the tower, but it was removed in 1940. The very attractive adjoining manse/rectory also dates from 1900.

A former layout.

Irishtown - St Matthews

Situated on Church Avenue, the church was built in 1704, on Fitzwilliam land, and enlarged in 1879 with new transepts and chancel. Note the combined "hammer beam" and "scissor" roof trusses. The nave was reduced in size a few decades ago, by building a wall at the rear, and forming meeting rooms, etc.

There are three pairs of 1880's windows in the apse by Earley & Powell of Dublin. There is another pair of windows on the south side of the chancel, reputed to be by Mayer of Munich in 1899, depicting St Mark and St Matthew - St Matthew appears to have only one leg!

The tower houses a collection of eight bronze tubular bells, no longer used. Instead, a recording plays the Westminster tune on the quarter hour, although the Whittington tune is played just before church services.

Irishtown - Gospel Hall

This was St Matthews National School, built in 1904, and attached to the church opposite. Portmarnock red brick dressings in granite walls.

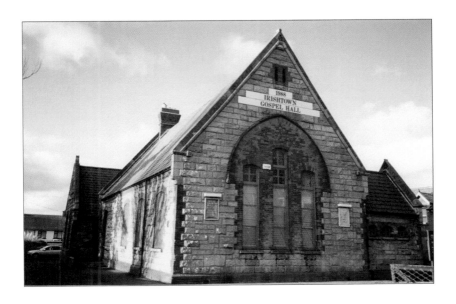

Killiney - Holy Trinity

The present Fitzpatricks Killiney Castle Hotel was once the home of Robert Warren, and he donated the adjoining plot for a church, and substantially funded the building project.

The church opened in 1859 as a Trustee Church, with capacity for 250 people, but transepts were added four years later. The gallery was removed in 1927.

There is a 1919 Harry Clarke stained glass lancet window in the nave, entitled "Angel of Peace & Hope". In 1945 a two-light window by H. V. McGoldrick (of Upper Pembroke Street) was installed.

Very pronounced "scissor" roof trusses.

Kilternan - St Tiernan

Near the turn-off for Ballycorus Road (going to the lead mines and chimney), this attractive small church, built with granite, dates from 1826, and is the work of renowned architect, John Semple.

New pews were installed in 1899, and the gallery was replaced in 1908. Mostly English stained glass.

Large "diaphragm" roof trusses spring from low level corbels, but these are timber framed, plastered to resemble masonry.

Kinsealy - St Doulagh

Located on the Malahide Road, one of the treasures of north Dublin, dating from the 12th and 13th centuries, this is more of a small monastery than a church, containing an oratory, Prior's chamber, library, refectory (diningroom), dormitory, and of course a cell for the hermit, St Doulagh. The crenellated tower reminds us that such places needed to be fortified in those days. In the yard, there are two small stone buildings, one being a well or baptistry, and the other called St Catherines Pond, a type of holy well. There is also an ancient stone cross. In the 1860's, major restoration, including a new nave, was completed.

123

124

Leeson Park - Christ Church

This imposing church was built in 1874 for the Church of Ireland, with granite exterior and limestone dressings. There are steep galleries in both transepts, and one at the rear. In the 1970's the Methodist congregation in Dublin was dwindling, resulting in the closure of many of their churches, which because of their small size, were often put to commercial use. In 1972, the Methodists reached an accord with their Church of Ireland colleagues, to share Leeson Park for Sunday Services. In 2005, the Church of Ireland moved out, the Methodists moved to nearby Wesley Hall, and this beautiful building is now home to the Romanian Orthodox Church – "Exaltation of the Holy Cross".

There is a lot of stained glass, much of it by Heaton Butler and Bayne of England, and some from An Tur Gloinne. Note the War Memorial Celtic cross outside the south-west of the church, and name-call plaque in the south transept.

Present iconostasis for the Romanian Orthodox service

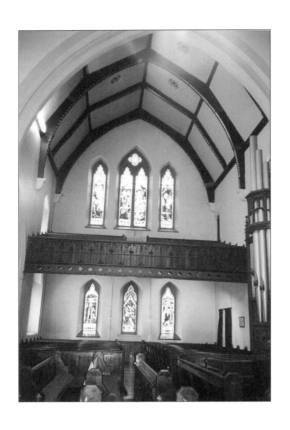

Previous layout

129

Leixlip - St Marys

15th century, with 12th century and earlier origins. Major restoration in 17th century.

Lucan - St Andrews

This church was built on the lands of famous architect, James Gandon, in 1823, at a cost of £2,307.

The Prayer table/altar is in the centre of north wall (instead of the east wall), which allows the congregation to participate more fully.

Malahide - St Andrews

Situated on Church Road, the church dates from 1829, to a John Semple design, but extended and re-arranged in 1869 by Welland & Gillespie.

"Suffer the Little Children" stained glass window by Catherine O'Brien. "Crucifixion" in original east window, by Kempe of London. Unusually for a Protestant church, there is no WW1 memorial. Graceful "arch brace" trusses support the roof.

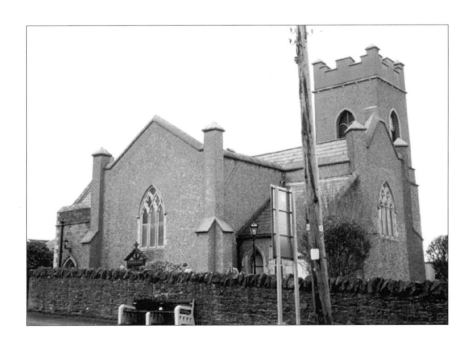

135

Milltown - St Philips

Located on Temple Road, off the Dartry Road, the church was built in 1840, and not consecrated until 1867, with the south aisle added in 1879. The tower was never finished. Note the "hammer beam" roof trusses. Some stained glass windows by Sillery, Dublin.

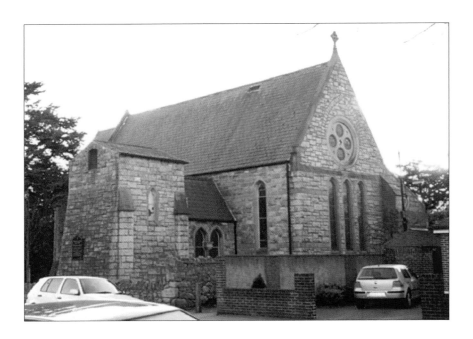

Monkstown

John Semple surpassed himself when he re-designed this beautiful granite church, at Monkstown Crescent, which opened in 1825. In fact, this building is a reconstruction/modification of an 1789 church. The fan vaulted ceilings are a unique and beautiful feature.

140

Mount Merrion - St Thomas

Built in 1874, at the bottom of Fosters Avenue, as a Chapel-of-Ease to the parish of Taney. Various small extensions were added over the years. Holds about 160 people, thereby making it small and cosy. Some nice stained glass windows by L. Lobin of France, Evie Hone, and A.E. Child.

Became a separate parish in 1956, and now grouped with St Philip and St James in Cross Avenue.

Mount Street Crescent - St Stephens

Designed by John Bowden, and after his death, by Joseph Welland. A rectangular building, consecrated in 1824, as a chapel of ease in the parish of St Peter. The sanctuary extended towards the canal in 1852, including an apse. Known t as the "Pepper Canister". The 1754 organ by John Snetzler

Mulhuddart - St Thomas

Consecrated in 1871, and designed by Welland & Gillespie. Even today, it is lit by candles, since there is no electricity (nor water). The bell in the tower is still rung before services, an uncommon practice nowadays. The church is located in Alderwood.

"Scissor" roof truss.

146

Naas - St Davids

The tower and possibly parts of the main fabric are reputed to date from around 1600, although the church was rebuilt in 1830. The bell dates from 1674. A combination collar and king post truss supports the roof.

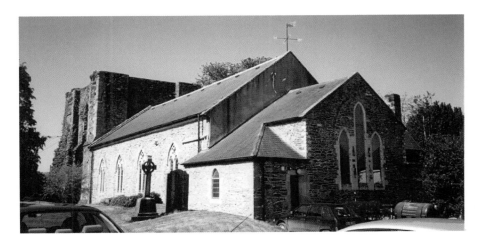

148

Newcastle Lyons - St Finians

This medieval church has an interesting older tower house attached. A bellcote is incorporated into the top of this tower, and the bell is still rung. The present nave is only about half the length of the original, since part of the roof has been removed, and a new east gable wall built.

North Strand Road

The North Strand Episcopal Church was opened in 1838, at a cost of £4,162. There are galleries on three sides. The Trustee status was vested in the RCB in 1891.

The original pulpit was at a height in the centre of the east wall – in effect the centre of attraction.

Ornate "queen post" roof trusses are a special feature.

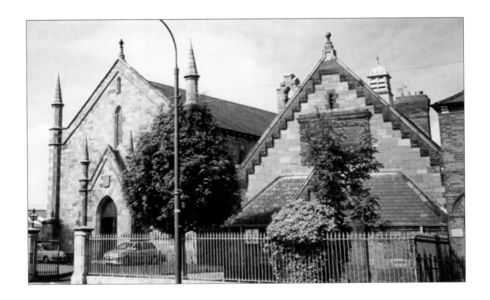

Parnell Square - Abbey

This landmark Presbyterian church, with its 180 foot spire, in also known as Findlaters Church, because it was paid for by the wealthy merchant, Alex Findlater, whose shops would later occupy most suburbs of Dublin. The church was built in 1864, although traces its origins to Mary's Abbey, off Capel Street. The large basement is used for concerts and social events

The 2,000 pipe organ occupies a prominent position in the chancel, and dates from 1912. Painted and coloured glass is used in the large north and south windows.

Pearse Street - St Marks

St Marks Anglican church was built in the 1750's, and is where Oscar Wilde was baptised in 1854. It was sold to nearby Trinity College in 1971, for use as an overflow library and exam hall. It was acquired in 1987 by a Pentecostal church, and is now called St Mark's Family Worship Centre. The tower at the west end was never completed.

156

Raheny - All Saints

Lord Ardilaun, Arthur Edward Guinness, lived in the 500 acre St Anne's estate, and he offered to pay for a new church within his estate, on condition that he be allowed to nominate the clergy, which practice continued up to 1938 – in most other Anglican churches, the annually elected Select Vestry chooses the rector. The exquisite church was built in 1889 by Collen Bros of Dublin and Portadown, to a design by George C. Ashlin. However, the steeple is the work of A. V. Sharpe of Great Brunswick Street (now called Pearse Street), as is the baptismal font, pulpit and oak seats. Ashlar granite is used externally, with limestone dressings, and the roof is covered with green Westmoreland slates, with fishscale coursing. Internally, the walls are lined with Bath stone, and various Irish marbles are used in the miniature attached columns. Irish oak is used in parts of the floor. Pitch pine is used to line the underside of the roof, between the "arch brace" roof trusses. Stained glass windows are in abundance, mostly by Heaton Butler & Bayne of London. The church was designed to hold 150 people, and it is only 80 foot by 52 foot, and 40 foot high, with a 110 feet high spire. The Guinness tiny gate lodge is also a gem.

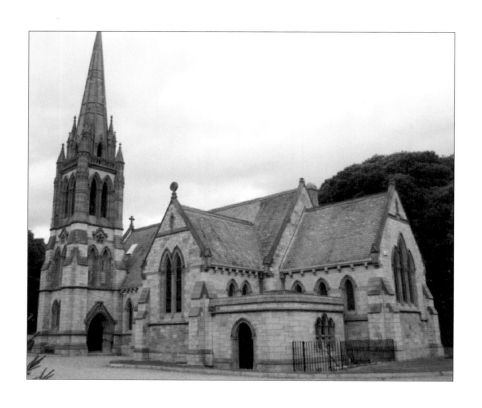

Ranelagh - Sandford

Built in 1826 as a trustee "chapel of ease" of the large St Peters parish, the church is named after the benefactor George Sandford of Somerset, who was a friend of Robert Newenham, one of the first trustees. The church was not an "established" church (financially supported by the Crown – every taxpayer), and so depended on pew rents. The latter were annual subscriptions for the right to occupy the same seat or pew at each service.

The original church was big, with a capacity of 700. It was enlarged in 1861 by extending 25 feet to the front, and building the present interesting façade. A further extension in 1880 to create a square building increased the capacity to 1,000 – a reflection of the popularity of great preachers. In 1906, the church gave up its trustee status, to become a parish church, under the umbrella of the Representative Church Body. Has 1927 two-light Harry Clarke window. Unusual type of "king post" roof trusses to nave, and "queen post" trusses to the aisles.

Rathfarnham

This rambling but attractive church was built in 1789, with the porch, tower and vestry added in 1821, the south transept and gallery added in 1852, and the north transept in 1889.

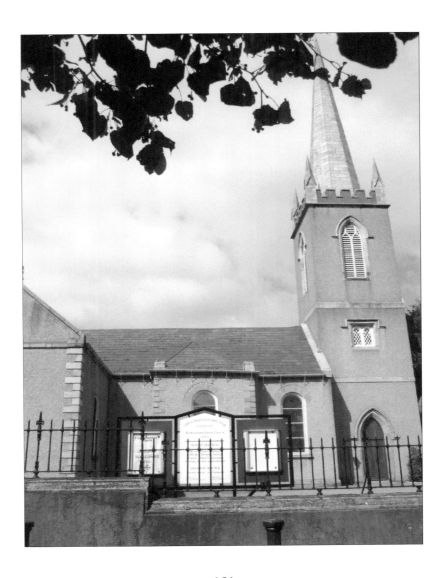

Rathgar - Christ Church

The original church was officially opened in 1862, but was greatly extended on most sides in 1901, including the very shallow transepts. As befits the Presbyterian tradition, a Scottish architect, Andrew Heiton from Perth, was the original designer, and Gilbert Cockburn was the builder. The elevations are in granite, with Portland stone dressings. The ground floor is in fact a large lecture hall, and the church proper on the upper level, is accessed by external steps. The lovely organ is shaped to fit around the base of the plain east rose window. A rear gallery is provided. There are a few stained glass windows, including a 1916 one by Geddes. Note the sub-divided pews.

Both "scissor" and "arch brace" roof trusses are used.

Rathgar - Zion

Nothing at all to do with the nearby Stratford College, a Jewish school, this Anglican church was built in 1861, to a design by Joseph Welland. Stockbroker, John Gould of Cullenswood, left his estate for building the church, which cost £10,000. Trustee status was ended in 1921 when the RCB took control.

This is a large building, intended to seat 850, with a lofty bell tower at the north-east corner. The north transept has been converted into commercial offices, called Zion Court. Limestone is the exterior material, with Portland stone dressings – note the clasping buttresses at the corners. Zion National School is alongside.

There are some stained glass windows, including a nice two-light one by A.E. Child in 1932, on the north of the nave.

165

Both "scissor" and "arch brace" roof trusses are used.

Rathgar - Methodist

The Methodist church in Brighton Road was built in 1874, although the transepts date from 1924, being a War Memorial project. The small spire dates from 1893.

James Joyce was born nearby in 41 Brighton Square in 1882.

Rathmichael

All this part of Loughlinstown was the land of Sir Charles Domville (who resided in Santry Court), and he donated the site – in fact he travelled over here for services.

This little granite gem was designed by Deane & Woodward in the Hiberno-Romanesque style – hence the round headed windows, and inclined door jambs. The 100-seater building opened in 1864, comprising a nave and chancel. The north aisle was added in 1904, separated from the original nave by pillars.

"Scissor" roof trusses used. The choir seats are at the rear beside the organ. Some windows by A. E. Child of An Tur Gloinne in the chancel, and also some gold coloured mosaic wall and floor tiles.

Vestry

Note the hand-operated bellows on the right at the base of the organ.

Rathmines - Grosvenor Baptist

Built by the Baptists in 1859, in Grosvenor Place, but sold to Plymouth Brethren five years later. Re-occupied by Baptists in 1942. There is a sunken and tiled immersion pool under the stage, for adult baptisms. Windows are plain, with no stained glass.

Former layout

Rathmines - Holy Trinity

Another little masterpiece by architect John Semple, this Anglican church, in Church Avenue, dates from 1828. Aisles and transepts added in 1863. Subdivided in recent years to allow for other activities, and a smaller congregation. Michael Healy window from 1909 in north transept.

Mock west wall.

Rush - Kenure

Built in 1866, by Sir W.H.R. Palmer. Granite exterior with sandstone bands. Fairfaced (unplastered) brickwork internally, with different band courses and arches.

St Stephens Green - Unitarian

This attractive granite building, with 97 foot spire, was built in 1863 by Hammond of Dublin and Drogheda, at a cost of £5,000. There are only two Unitarian Churches in Ireland, and they practice a liberal Christian faith. The famous Damer Hall in the semi-basement staged Irish language theatre productions in the 1950's to the 1970's, including the premiere of "An Giall" (The Hostage), by Brendan Behan, in 1957.

The interior is L-shaped, with a north-south nave, east aisle, and large north-east transept. There are many stained glass windows, including the main north window from 1918 by Alfred Ernest Child. Opposite the blank transept window is a large window, with tracery and coloured glass, in memory of the Hutton family, famous Dublin coach builders.

178

Sandymount - Christ Church

Built by the Methodists in 1857, but shared with Presbyterians since 1975.

Sandymount - St John the Evangelist

This landmark trustee church in Park Avenue was opened in 1850, and designed by Benjamin Ferrey. Polygonal granite facades, with soft Caen sandstone dressings from France. "Hammerbeam" trusses support the roof. Some stained glass windows from the studio of Joshua Clarke & Sons.

In Anglican circles, this congregation is regarded as "High Church", or Anglo-Catholic, that is, more Catholic than Protestant. They burn incense during services, and have the only set of Stations of the Cross" in the Church of Ireland.

Note the carved heads under the gutter.

Santry - St Pappan

Situated on Church Lane, off the Swords, Road, the church dates from 1780, but was restored a century later. Some nice stained glass windows from An Tur Gloinne in the 1920/30's. Sir Compton Domville mausoleum in graveyard.

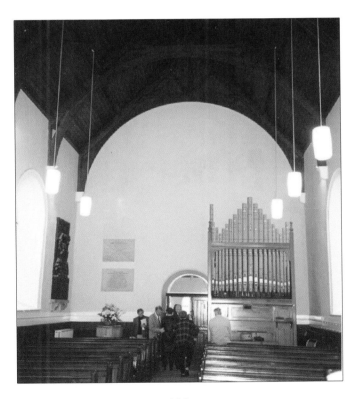

Skerries - Holmpatrick

This interesting little church was built on elevated ground donated by the local landlord, the Hamilton family, to a design by James Rogers, and was consecrated in 1868. The Woods family were intermarried with the Hamiltons, and so various windows and plaques are in memory of the Woods. Some plaques came from the old church, which was built in 1720.

The west rose window, by Mayer of Munich, dates from 1894, and depicts the Resurrection. The main east window above the altar consists of coloured glass and coat-of-arms of the Woods family.

The roof trusses are very unusual, consisting of "king-rods" in an "arch brace" assembly.

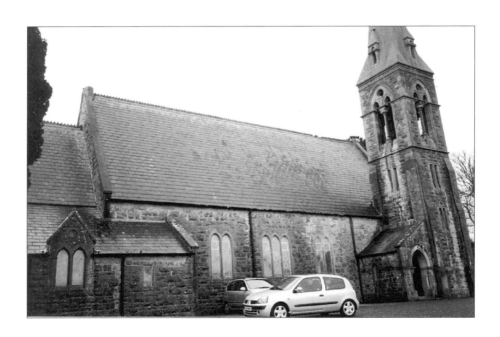

SCR - Dublin Mosque

This former Donore Presbyterian church beside the National Stadium on the South Circular Road dates from 1881, and was converted into a mosque in 1983. The seats were removed, and a prayer niche and pulpit formed in the centre of the east wall, facing Mecca, since, unusually, the original orientation of the church was not east-west. The exterior is in granite, with sandstone dressings, especially the feature rose window. The roof is supported on a variation of the "hammer beam" truss, although these are supplemented with a ceiling tie-rod, and a centre hanging rod. The women's balcony is along the west and north.

Stillorgan - St Brigids

This church, on Church Road, near Glenalbyn Sports Centre, was built in the period 1706 to 1712, although the tower and north aisle were added later in 1812.

A gallery at the rear and to the side increases capacity, and the boxed pews in the nave are still in use. The main east window has some lovely stained glass, although a nearby smaller window is also beautiful. Note the flat plain ceiling, in contrast to many more modern churches, where the roof trusses are a special feature.

Famous names associated with this old church include Archbishop Richard Whately, artist William Orpen, and Sir Hugh Gough.

Straffan, Co Kildare

Straffan estate was owned by the Henry family, until purchased by Hugh Barton in 1830, and he paid for the building of this church in 1833. Naturally there are some memorials to his family inside the church. The RCB assumed responsibility for the church in 1933.

There is a stained glass window by Catherine O'Brien, and three by A.E. Child, dating from the early 20th century. "Hammerbeam" type construction at base of roof, with a braced collar higher up.

Swords - St Columba

9th/10th century Round Tower, part of monastic settlement, and a 14th century square tower on its own, all on Church Road.

Cut granite church, 1818, on site of the old abbey. The east window in the sanctuary dates from 1818, and is by Joshua Bradley.

Tallaght - St Maelruain

This church is located on the Old Blessington Road, to the west of the Priory.

The beautiful church, built with black calp limestone, has John Semple written all over it, and dates back to 1829. The adjoining tower (now used as a vestry) was part of a medieval church.

The massive internal "diaphragm" arches supporting the roof are a feature, extending low down to corbels near the base of the buttressed walls, and picking them out in bright colours was an inspired idea. However, the trusses are apparently timber framed, plastered to resemble masonry.

Taney - Christ Church

St Nahi's church, the original parish church, is still under the Luas cable-stayed Dargan Bridge in Dundrum. However, an expanding population necessitated the building of a much bigger church on Taney Road, which opened in 1818, although not finished. A lot of alterations and extensions were carried out over the years, including re-arrangement of the basic layout. Most external walls are of squared coursed limestone, although there are areas of polygonal granite, and smooth render. Mostly English stained glass.

Since 2000, the tower has housed the original 1828 bells from St Georges in Hardwicke Street (beside Temple St Childrens Hospital)

199

Terenure - Synagogue

This Jewish synagogue was built in 1953, although refurbished in 1967 after a fire, at which stage, stained glass windows were installed in both the north and south walls - the north one depicts the Old City of Jerusalem, while the south one depicts ten different religious festivals.

It is located on the Rathfarnham Road, just south of Terenure village.

View from women's gallery

The Ark, where the Torah Scrolls are housed.

Stained glass window of Jerusalem, showing the former Temple Mount (with Golden Gate in the east old city wall), and Wailing Wall to the left.

Thomas Street - St Catherine

Opened in 1769 after rebuilding, on part of the site of the old St Thomas Abbey. Classical facade faces north. Closed in 1966, and now used by CORE, an Anglican off-shoot.

Tullow

This granite Anglican church, on Brighton Road near Foxrock, was consecrated in 1864, and was designed by Welland & Gillespie.

In 1904, the original east-west nave was converted to transepts, and a new nave and chancel built.

Catherine O'Brien and Beatrice Elvery provided the stained glass windows.

The War Memorial Plaque is on the exterior, to the right of the porch, probably more sensible than being on the inside.

Werburgh Street - St Werburghs

This church, which was the original Chapel Royal for the adjoining Dublin Castle, dates from 1719, although was extensively restored after a fire in the 1750's. The spire was removed in 1810, and the tower, including six bells, was removed in 1836.

Dean Jonathan Swift, the author of "Gulliver's Travels", was baptised here, and Lord Edward Fitzgerald is buried in the vaults.

Whitechurch

John Semple's church, which dates from 1827, is probably well known to ramblers in the adjoining Marley Park, since the lovely slender spire can be seen from afar. The church was built on part of the old Marley estate, then owned by John David LaTouche.

A gallery was added in 1834 (extended in 1993), and the chancel and vestry date from 1868. Timber framed diaphragm arches, plastered to look like masonry, support the roof. Interestingly, the adjoining school pre-dates the church by four years.

209

Selected Sources

Much information of a historical nature was obtained from pamphlets and leaflets produced by numerous parishes, in addition to their websites.

www.gloine.ie   This is a valuable online database of stained glass in Church of Ireland buildings.

N.I.A.H.   National Inventory of Architectural Heritage has some information concerning the age of buildings.

"Times, Chimes and Charms of Dublin", 2nd Edition, 2010, by Joe Curtis, has some information on church bells and public clocks.

Acknowledgements

Many thanks to the clergy of all denominations, too numerous to mention by name, who gave me permission to take photos, and allowed me to look around such wonderful places of worship.

Other books by the same author

Times, Chimes & Charms of Dublin (2nd Edition, 2010)

Harolds Cross (3rd Edition, reprinted 2009)

Harolds Cross in Old Photos, 2011

Mount Merrion, 1711-2011

Mount Merrion in old photos, 2012

Great Landmarks in Time, 1999

Haslam's Gold, 2009

Ferdie and Toots, 2011

Truly I tell you, 2012

Printed in Poland
by Amazon Fulfillment
Poland Sp. z o.o., Wrocław

54042158R00126